HOW TO SURVIVE ANYTHING!

GIRLS ONLY

SCHOLASTIC INC.

NEW YORK • TORONTO • LONDON • AUCKLAND
SYDNEY • MEXICO CITY • NEW DELHI • HONG KONG

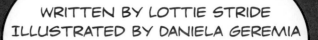

WRITTEN BY LOTTIE STRIDE
ILLUSTRATED BY DANIELA GEREMIA

EDITED BY BRYONY JONES
DESIGNED BY ZOE QUAYLE

DISCLAIMER

The publisher and author disclaim, as far as is legally permissible, all liability for accidents, injuries, or loss that may occur as a result of information or instructions given in this book. Use your best common sense at all times – particularly when using heat or sharp objects – always wear appropriate safety gear, stay within the law and local rules, and be considerate of other people. Always remember to ask a responsible adult for assistance and take their advice whenever necessary.

ISBN 978-0-545-43095-1

First published in Great Britain in 2011 by Buster Books, an imprint of Michael O'Mara Books Limited.

10 9 8 7 6 5 4 3 2 1   12 13 14 15 16

Printed in the USA   40
First American edition, May 2012

CONTENTS

WARNING!

NOT READING THIS BOOK COULD SERIOUSLY CRAMP YOUR STYLE.

HOW WOULD YOU DEAL IF YOU WERE ASKED TO MAKE A SPEECH TO A ROOM FULL OF PEOPLE? WHAT WOULD YOU DO IF YOU WERE FACED WITH A ZOMBIE ATTACK? HOW WOULD YOU REACT IF YOU HAD A HUGE FIGHT WITH YOUR BEST FRIEND?

THIS FABULOUS BOOK WILL SHOW YOU HOW TO SURVIVE ANYTHING LIFE THROWS AT YOU IN THE MOST STYLISH WAY POSSIBLE.

WHETHER IT'S THE LITTLE THINGS IN LIFE, LIKE CHOOSING THE RIGHT PAIR OF SUNGLASSES, OR THE STRANGER THINGS, SUCH AS ENCOUNTERING ALIENS, THIS BOOK WILL TELL YOU WHAT TO DO, AND HOW TO LOOK GOOD DOING IT.

ARE YOU READY?

BEING A CHAMPION MEANS BEING PREPARED FOR EVEN THE MOST UNEXPECTED OF CHALLENGES. FOLLOW THESE TIPS TO MAKE SURE YOU'LL MAKE IT TO #1.

BE A WINNER

- WHEN FACED WITH DANGER, FOLLOW YOUR INSTINCTS.
- DON'T FREAK! EVEN THE MOST GLAMOROUS GALS HAVE BAD HAIR DAYS.
- HARD WORK AND PRACTICE ARE GUARANTEED TO PAY OFF.
- BE CONFIDENT, BECAUSE PEOPLE LIKE YOU FOR YOU.

BE UTTERLY FABULOUS

- DON'T FOLLOW THE CROWD — CREATE YOUR OWN LOOK.
- ACT CONFIDENT EVEN IF YOU DON'T ALWAYS FEEL IT.
- PUT YOUR BEST INTO EVERYTHING YOU DO, EVEN IF IT'S SOMETHING YOU'RE DREADING.
- TAKE RISKS EVEN IF THEY SCARE YOU.

SO WHAT ARE YOU WAITING FOR? TURN THE PAGE, READ, LEARN, AND WIN!

HOW TO SURVIVE A BFF FIGHT

ALL FRIENDS ARGUE SOMETIMES. HERE'S A GUIDE TO THE DOS AND DON'TS OF GETTING THROUGH EVEN THE BIGGEST FIGHT.

EXCLUDING HER IS NOT REALLY THE ANSWER.

WE'RE NOT TALKING TO HER. SHE'S NOT OUR FRIEND ANYMORE.

BESIDES, BEING IGNORED CAN WORK BOTH WAYS!

HEY, WHERE ARE YOU ALL GOING?

SULKING WON'T MAKE YOU FEEL BETTER.

AND BEING A DRAMA QUEEN WON'T FIX ANYTHING.

BESIDES, JUST THINK ABOUT ALL THE FUN YOU'VE HAD TOGETHER ...

HE'S SO CUTE!

... AND ALL THE SECRETS YOU'VE SHARED.

First panel caption: FIRST, WHY NOT ARRANGE TO MEET IN ONE OF YOUR FAVORITE PLACES?

THERE ARE TWO SIDES TO EVERY STORY, SO LISTEN TO EACH OTHER. IF IT HELPS, BRING A REFEREE.

YOU GET THREE MINUTES EACH. NO INTERRUPTING.

IF *YOU* WERE WRONG, ADMIT IT. SHOW HER YOU'RE SORRY.

Sorry! This is for you!

IF *SHE* WAS WRONG, ACCEPT HER APOLOGY AND BE GRACIOUS.

LET'S NEVER FIGHT AGAIN!

IF YOU FIND THAT YOU WERE *BOTH* WRONG, THERE'S ONLY ONE THING TO DO ...

... BECAUSE IT'S MUCH MORE FUN TO BE FRIENDS THAN ENEMIES.

THAT WAS DUMB.

HOW TO SURVIVE SOCCER TRYOUTS

HERE ARE SOME TOP TIPS TO HELP YOU ROCK THE TRYOUTS, AND MAKE THE TEAM.

1. DO THREE THINGS IN THE WEEK BEFORE TRYOUTS.

PRACTICE ...

PRACTICE ...

... AND PRACTICE!

2. GET A GOOD NIGHT'S SLEEP BEFORE TRYOUTS.

3. WARM-UPS WILL HELP YOUR GAME – SO GET TO TRYOUTS NICE AND EARLY.

OOH!

BUT DON'T GO OVERBOARD!

4. WEAR A UNIFORM THAT STANDS OUT FROM THE CROWD, IF YOU'RE ALLOWED TO. THIS WILL HELP THE COACH REMEMBER YOU.

5. PLAY AS WELL AS YOU CAN. MAKE EVERY EFFORT TO GET THE BALL.

FOUL!!

6. STAY CALM, WHATEVER HAPPENS.

OVER HERE!

8. AFTER THE GAME, TRY TO TALK TO THE COACH. BE POLITE – AND TELL HIM YOU HAD FUN.

7. COACHES LIKE TEAM PLAYERS, SO DON'T HOG THE BALL.

THANK YOU, I'D LOVE TO PLAY ON THE TEAM!

HOW TO SURVIVE A BREAKOUT

EVER WANTED TO BE ONE OF THOSE GIRLS WITH GLOWING SKIN?

IS THE REALITY DIFFERENT? DON'T PANIC! HERE'S HOW TO SURVIVE A BREAKOUT AND GET THE SKIN OF YOUR DREAMS.

WASH YOUR FACE AND KEEP IT CLEAN, SO YOUR PIMPLES DON'T GET ANY WORSE.

YAWN!

ALWAYS TAKE OFF YOUR MAKEUP BEFORE BED.

WHEN YOU TREAT YOUR PIMPLES, DAB ON SOME BLEMISH CREAM AND THEN LEAVE THEM ALONE.

NEVER, *EVER* SQUEEZE!

NOW THAT YOU KNOW HOW TO DEAL WITH A BREAKOUT, HERE ARE SOME TIPS TO TRY TO AVOID ONE IN THE FIRST PLACE.

... BUT PICK THE RIGHT MOISTURIZER FOR YOUR SENSITIVE, DRY, OR OILY SKIN.

MOISTURIZE WHENEVER YOUR SKIN FEELS DRY, EVEN IF IT'S PIMPLY ...

IT'S IMPORTANT TO BE HEALTHY. WHAT YOU PUT INSIDE SHOWS ON THE OUTSIDE, AND MIGHT HELP TO REDUCE THE CHANCE OF A BREAKOUT.

A BIT OF FRESH AIR IS GOOD FOR YOUR SKIN.

BUT DON'T FORGET TO TAKE CARE IN THE SUN.

CHOOSE AN OIL-FREE SUNSCREEN IF YOUR SKIN IS GREASY AND PRONE TO PIMPLES.

EXERCISE WILL ALSO HELP TO GIVE YOUR SKIN A GLOW.

AND IF YOU DON'T LIKE SPORTS, YOU CAN FIND OTHER WAYS TO EXERCISE.

GET PLENTY OF SLEEP.

BUT DON'T FORGET THAT SOMETIMES, IT'S OK TO BREAK THE RULES!

HOW TO SHOW YOU'RE SORRY

SOMETIMES, SAYING SORRY TO A FRIEND JUST DOESN'T SEEM LIKE ENOUGH.

SORRY!

THAT'S WHEN A SMALL GIFT CAN HELP. FIRST, THINK WHAT SHE WOULD REALLY LIKE AS A PRESENT.

LIP BALM!

MAKE IT YOURSELF, TO SHOW YOU'RE REALLY SORRY. HERE'S WHAT YOU NEED:

I TABLESPOON OF PETROLEUM JELLY	I TEASPOON OF HONEY

STIR THEM TOGETHER UNTIL THE BALM IS MIXED AND LOOKS SMOOTH. THEN PUT IT IN A SMALL JAR.

DON'T FORGET TO MAKE YOUR PRESENT AS BEAUTIFUL AS POSSIBLE!

WHY NOT ADD A PRETTY HANDWRITTEN LABEL OR A BOW?

THANKS! I FORGIVE YOU.

HOW TO HAVE THE BEST SLEEPOVER EVER

DO YOU WANT TO HOST THE BEST SLEEPOVER EVER?
READ ON TO FIND OUT HOW.

GIVE YOUR SLEEPOVER A THEME. IT COULD BE ANYTHING, FROM "PINK" TO "SPOOKY." DECORATE YOUR ROOM TO MAKE IT REALLY SPECIAL.

I PICKED HOLLYWOOD GLAMOUR!

YOUR GUESTS CAN DRESS UP IN FUN OUTFITS.

PLAN LOTS OF THINGS TO DO. A SLEEPOVER CAN BE THE PERFECT TIME TO EXPERIMENT WITH NEW LOOKS ...

... OR TO PAMPER YOURSELVES.

YOU COULD MAKE SOME GOOD EATS TOGETHER.

OR TEST YOUR DANCING SKILLS.

I'M WINNING!

DVDS ARE A SLEEPOVER STAPLE. HAVE A SELECTION READY TO SUIT THE MOOD.

TRY A ROM-COM ...

... A TEARJERKER ...

... OR A SCARY MOVIE, IF YOU'RE FEELING BRAVE.

REMIND YOUR GUESTS TO PACK WISELY.

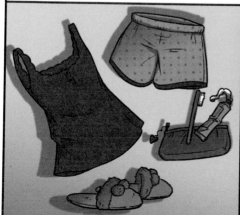

AND TO BRING SUPPLIES FOR THE MOST IMPORTANT PART OF THE SLEEPOVER ...

... THE LATE NIGHT SNACK!

HOW TO TAKE THE PERFECT SCHOOL PHOTO

DO YOU WANT TO LOOK YOUR VERY BEST FOR YOUR SCHOOL PHOTO?
FOLLOW OUR TIPS!

PREPARATIONS SHOULD NEVER BE RUSHED.

MAKE SURE YOUR SKIN IS SUPER-SOFT.

DON'T FORGET THAT SOME PLACES NEED A LITTLE EXTRA ATTENTION.

ENJOY GETTING READY. IF YOU'RE RELAXED, YOU'LL LOOK GREAT.

ALLOW PLENTY OF TIME FOR THOSE BIG DECISIONS.

LEARN THE THREE RULES FOR THE
PERFECT BLOW-DRY ...

1. FIRST, ADD BODY TO
THE ROOTS.

2. POINT THE
DRYER DOWN THE
LENGTH OF THE
HAIR TO ADD SHINE.

3. ONE FINAL COOL
BLAST FIXES THE STYLE.

... AND THE BEST WAY TO PAINT YOUR NAILS.

ALWAYS PAINT
TWO COATS!

1. PAINT ONE STRIPE
DOWN THE CENTER.

2. ONE DOWN THE
LEFT-HAND SIDE.

3. THEN ONE DOWN
THE RIGHT-HAND SIDE.

ACCESSORIES WILL REALLY
MAKE YOUR OUTFIT.

FINALLY, A CONFIDENT GIRL NEVER FORGETS
TO PRACTICE THE MOST IMPORTANT
THING OF ALL - A DAZZLING SMILE!

HOW TO SURVIVE BROTHERS

BROTHERS ARE STRANGE THINGS ...	... THEY HAVE ODD HABITS ...	... AND EAT WEIRD FOOD.

SO HERE'S HOW TO DEAL WITH THEM:

1. NEVER GO INTO YOUR BROTHER'S ROOM WITHOUT BEING FULLY PREPARED.

2. YOUR DIARY MUST BE PROTECTED AT ALL COSTS.

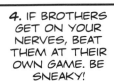

4. IF BROTHERS GET ON YOUR NERVES, BEAT THEM AT THEIR OWN GAME. BE SNEAKY!

TRY PUTTING HOT SAUCE IN THEIR DRINKS. DON'T TELL!

5. IF ALL ELSE FAILS, REMEMBER ONE THING: BROTHERS MIGHT HAVE ANNOYING FRIENDS ...

... OR THEY MIGHT NOT!

SCARY SURVIVAL DOS AND DON'TS

FOLLOW THE DOS AND DON'TS BELOW IF YOU HAPPEN TO FIND YOURSELF IN A MONSTROUS SITUATION.

1. YOUR FRIEND APPEARS TO HAVE FANGS. **DO** INVENT AN EXCUSE TO GO HOME IMMEDIATELY.

DON'T ASK HIM TO ADMIRE YOUR EARRINGS.

2. YOU WAKE TO FIND A GHOST IN YOUR BEDROOM. **DO** LET YOUR GHOST CHAT. IT IS PROBABLY JUST BORED AND LONELY.

DON'T THROW THINGS OR YELL AT YOUR GHOST. IT MAY REACT BADLY.

3. AN ALIEN SPACESHIP LANDS IN THE PARK. **DO** SEIZE THE CHANCE FOR A FRONT-PAGE SCOOP.

DON'T SNEEZE AT THE WRONG MOMENT. IF THE ALIENS NOTICE YOU, THEY MAY TAKE YOU BACK TO THEIR HOME PLANET.

HOW TO HANDLE BECOMING RICH

IT'S GREAT NEWS WHEN YOU COME INTO SOME MONEY YOU'RE NOT EXPECTING. THE NEW CASH CAN GIVE YOU SOME FUN DECISIONS TO MAKE.

SHOULD I SAVE IT?

OR SPEND IT?

BUT SUPPOSE YOUR WACKY GREAT-UNCLE LEAVES YOU A FORTUNE. WHAT THEN?

HE LEFT ME ALL OF HIS MONEY? JUST ME?

WHEN YOU ARE RICH, YOU MAY FIND YOU BECOME A BIT OF A CELEBRITY. BE CAREFUL – TALK SHOWS CAN BE DAUNTING FOR A BEGINNER ...

FIRST, DON'T CELEBRATE TO EXCESS.

OVERNIGHT, THE RICHEST GIRL IN THE WORLD!

... SO INVEST IN SOME MEDIA TRAINING.

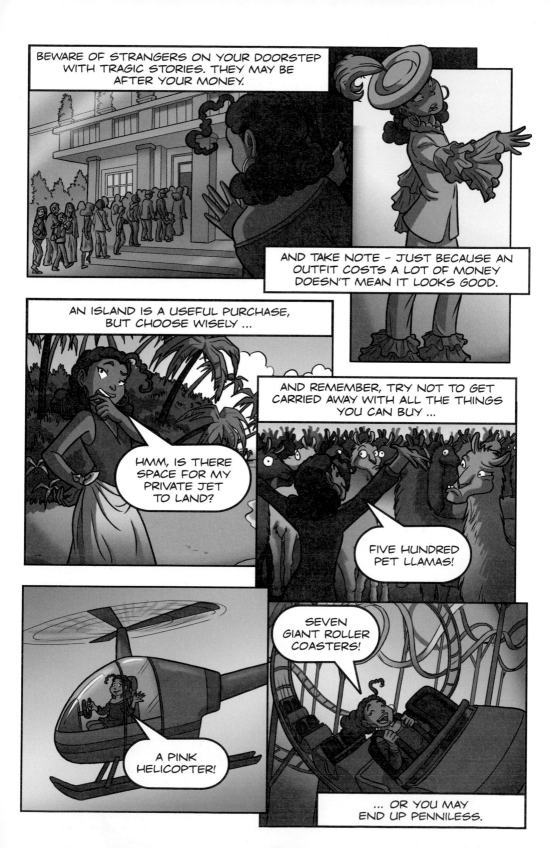

HOW TO KEEP STUFF SECRET

SOMETIMES GIRLS NEED TO PASS ON VITAL SECRET INFORMATION.

BEWARE! ENEMIES MAY BE LURKING AROUND EVERY CORNER ...

... READY TO STEAL YOUR SECRETS.

BUT EVERY SPY HAS A SECRET WEAPON – INVISIBLE INK.

HERE'S HOW YOU MAKE IT.

MIX TOGETHER EQUAL AMOUNTS OF WATER AND BAKING SODA. YOU ONLY NEED A LITTLE OF BOTH!

THERE'S NOTHING HERE.

DIP A TOOTHPICK IN THE MIXTURE AND WRITE YOUR MESSAGE.

A COTTON SWAB WORKS, TOO.

THEN PASS IT ON TO A GIRL IN THE KNOW, WHO CAN REVEAL YOUR SECRET MESSAGE USING THE HEAT FROM A HAIR DRYER!

INVISIBLE INK ISN'T PRACTICAL IN EVERY SITUATION. SOMETIMES A SECRET CODE IS BEST.

HERE'S A SIMPLE ONE TO GET YOU STARTED - TRY USING SYMBOLS INSTEAD OF PHRASES.

AFTERNOON

CRUSH

TOMORROW

TO DISCUSS

MEET ME

SECRET

CAN YOU UNLOCK THE MESSAGE IN THE NOTE?

OF COURSE, SOMETIMES IT'S BETTER NOT TO WRITE ANYTHING DOWN AT ALL. WHY NOT CHOOSE HAND SIGNALS OR BODY MOVEMENTS TO CONVEY INFORMATION INSTANTLY?

SCRATCH!

YAWN!

MEANS: I'M BORED - LET'S LEAVE IMMEDIATELY.

MEANS: DON'T LOOK - HE'S BEHIND YOU.

MEANS: LET'S CHANGE LOCATION.

MEANS: SOMEONE'S LISTENING TO OUR CONVERSATION.

IT'S NEARLY TEST TIME, AND YOU NEED TO STUDY. DON'T PANIC, JUST FOLLOW THESE TIPS.

1. GIVE YOURSELF PLENTY OF TIME. IF YOU LEAVE ALL YOUR STUDYING TO THE NIGHT BEFORE ...

... YOU MAY REGRET IT.

2. CHOOSE WHERE YOU STUDY CAREFULLY. SOME PLACES ARE BETTER THAN OTHERS - A QUIET ROOM AND A CLEAR DESK IS FAR BETTER THAN A ROOM WHERE THE TV IS BLARING AND THE DOG IS BARKING.

3. LOOK AT YOUR TEST TIMETABLE AND ASK YOURSELF SOME QUESTIONS, THEN PLAN YOUR STUDYING AHEAD. IT HELPS YOU TO KNOW WHAT YOU NEED TO STUDY EACH DAY.

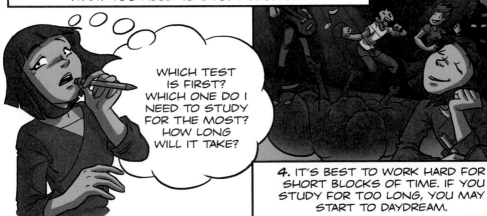

WHICH TEST IS FIRST? WHICH ONE DO I NEED TO STUDY FOR THE MOST? HOW LONG WILL IT TAKE?

4. IT'S BEST TO WORK HARD FOR SHORT BLOCKS OF TIME. IF YOU STUDY FOR TOO LONG, YOU MAY START TO DAYDREAM.

5. WHEN YOU TAKE A BREAK, DO SOMETHING COMPLETELY DIFFERENT.

BUT DON'T LET YOURSELF GET DISTRACTED FOR TOO LONG.

6. THERE ARE LOTS OF DIFFERENT WAYS TO STUDY.

TIME TO DO A PRACTICE TEST.

I'LL ASK YOU QUESTIONS FIRST, THEN YOU ASK ME.

AND IT CAN HELP TO SWITCH FROM ONE SUBJECT TO ANOTHER, SO YOU DON'T GET BORED.

TIME FOR SOME MATH NOW.

7. IF YOU LET YOUR FAMILY KNOW WHEN YOU'RE WORKING, THEY CAN BE SUPPORTIVE.

8. REMEMBER, JUST DO THE BEST YOU CAN, AND AFTER YOUR TESTS ARE OVER, HAVE FUN!

HOW TO SURVIVE SHYNESS

INVITATION TO MY BIRTHDAY

BUT THE ONLY PERSON YOU'LL KNOW IS THE BIRTHDAY GIRL.

KEEP CALM. JUST SMILE AND ACT FRIENDLY AND OTHER PEOPLE WILL WANT TO TALK TO YOU. THE KEY IS TO MAKE EYE CONTACT.

HI, I'M ALLISON.

NO ONE FINDS NEW FRIENDS ON THE FLOOR. LOOK UP AND AROUND.

AND REMEMBER, YOU PROBABLY WON'T BE THE ONLY SHY GIRL THERE.

HI!

HI!

IF YOU SEE SOMEONE ELSE ON THEIR OWN, BE BRAVE AND SAY HELLO.

A COMPLIMENT IS A GOOD WAY TO START A CONVERSATION.

I LIKE YOUR SHIRT.

ALTHOUGH TOO MANY MAY MAKE YOU LOOK A BIT STRANGE.

YOUR HAIR IS AMAZING.

I LOVE YOUR NAIL POLISH.

THOSE SHOES ARE SO COOL.

QUESTIONS ARE A GOOD WAY TO BREAK THE ICE. DON'T WORRY, THERE ARE LOTS OF THINGS YOU COULD ASK ABOUT.

FAMILY? HOBBIES? FAVORITE CLASSES?

YOU CAN ASK A QUESTION LIKE ...

DO YOU WATCH REALITY TV?

YES.

... BUT QUESTIONS THAT START WITH WHO, WHAT, OR WHERE ARE EVEN BETTER, BECAUSE THEY NEED MORE THAN A ONE-WORD ANSWER.

WHAT'S YOUR FAVORITE SHOW?

BEFORE YOU KNOW IT, YOU'LL BE CHATTING AWAY.

HA HA!

HA HA!

HOW TO HANDLE SUDDEN STARDOM

DO YOU FEEL LIKE YOU'RE ON THE BRINK OF BECOMING FAMOUS?
HERE ARE A FEW TIPS ON HOW TO HANDLE SUDDEN STARDOM.

INVENT A DAZZLING AUTOGRAPH. SHORTEN YOUR
NAME, SHOWBIZ-STYLE, AND ADD SOME SWIRLS.

BUT BEWARE, YOU MAY
BE ASKED TO SIGN
SOME STRANGE
THINGS.

IF YOUR WRIST GETS TIRED FROM SIGNING ...

... STRAP IT UP AND ADD SOME BLING!

LOOK LIKE A
STAR WITH ALL
THE RIGHT
ACCESSORIES.

MORE STARDOM SURVIVAL TIPS

YOU KNOW WHAT TO DO WHEN STARDOM STRIKES –
HERE'S WHAT **NOT** TO DO!

I ASKED FOR PINK SLIPPERS. HOW DARE YOU BRING ME THESE?

WHERE ARE MY SIX HEART-SHAPED ICE CUBES?

SCHOOLWORK IS NOT FOR SUPERSTARS!

I ONLY EAT BROCCOLI WHEN IT'S A FULL MOON!

REMEMBER, DIVA-LIKE BEHAVIOR MIGHT GET YOU INTO THE PAGES OF A GOSSIP MAGAZINE, BUT FOR ALL THE **WRONG** REASONS.

HOW TO SURVIVE A CAMPING TRIP

CAMPING MAY NOT ALWAYS BE A GIRL'S TOP CHOICE FOR A VACATION.

BUT HERE'S HOW TO MAKE THE BEST OF IT.

CAMPING IS AN OUTDOOR ACTIVITY – SO PACK CAREFULLY FOR **ALL** WEATHER.

BE POSITIVE! REMEMBER, BAD WEATHER CAN'T LAST FOREVER.

WOW, WHAT A NICE SUNRISE!

BESIDES, FRESH AIR IS EXCELLENT FOR THE SKIN. AND A BRISK WALK IS A GREAT WORKOUT.

THE NIGHTS CAN GET EXTRA CHILLY, SO BRING WARM LAYERS ...

... AND A FLASHLIGHT.

WHOOPS!

BUT DON'T FORGET, NIGHTTIME CAN ALSO BE THE BEST PART OF THE TRIP!

HOW TO SURVIVE A FASHION DISASTER

IT'S PARTY TIME – AND YOU HAVE *NOTHING TO WEAR.*

MOM'S NO HELP.

YOU'VE GOT LOTS OF CLOTHES!

NEITHER IS YOUR BROTHER.

NO LOANS!

AND DON'T EVEN BOTHER ASKING YOUR SISTER.

NO, NO, NO.

IT'S TIME TO GET CREATIVE!

SOME FABRIC GLUE AND A FEW SEQUINS OR BEADS CAN TURN THIS ...

... INTO THIS.

OR GIVE A WHOLE NEW LOOK TO A SKIRT YOU NO LONGER LIKE.

AND FABRIC PENS CAN TURN A PLAIN T-SHIRT ...

SLIP A PIECE OF CARD INSIDE TO STOP INK RUNNING FROM THE FRONT TO THE BACK.

... INTO A PARTY T-SHIRT. VOILÀ!

SET YOUR PATTERN BY IRONING IT ON.

ALWAYS BE CAREFUL WHEN YOU USE AN IRON. ASK AN ADULT TO HELP.

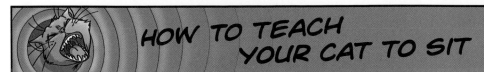

HOW TO TEACH YOUR CAT TO SIT

HAVE YOU ALWAYS WANTED A DOG, BUT BEEN UNABLE TO PERSUADE YOUR PARENTS? NEVER FEAR – TRY TEACHING YOUR CAT THIS TRICK INSTEAD.

MANY PEOPLE THINK THAT THEIR FELINE FRIENDS ARE TOO INDEPENDENT TO LEARN TRICKS.

BUT THAT'S NOT TRUE. YOU REALLY **CAN** TEACH YOUR CAT TO SIT. HERE'S HOW.

1. BEFORE YOU START, MAKE SURE YOUR CAT IS FEELING RELAXED, SO THAT IT WILL BE MORE WILLING TO LEARN.

2. SHOW YOUR CAT AN EDIBLE REWARD, SUCH AS A CAT TREAT, AND SAY, *"INSERT YOUR CAT'S NAME HERE – SIT."*

3. MOVE THE TREAT BACKWARD OVER YOUR CAT'S HEAD. AS IT WATCHES THE TREAT, IT SHOULD SIT DOWN TO BALANCE.

IF IT DOESN'T, GENTLY PRESS DOWN ON ITS HINDQUARTERS. DON'T PUSH TOO HARD, OR YOUR CAT MIGHT GET ANGRY.

4. AS YOUR CAT SITS, GIVE IT LOTS OF PRAISE, AND, OF COURSE, A TREAT - OR MORE IF YOU FEEL LIKE IT.

YOU MIGHT GET BETTER RESULTS IF YOU TRAIN YOUR CAT WHEN IT'S HUNGRY.

IF YOU FIND THAT EITHER YOU OR THE CAT IS BECOMING FRUSTRATED, LEAVE IT UNTIL ANOTHER TIME.

BE PATIENT, AND KEEP PRACTICING.

WITH TIME AND PRACTICE, YOUR CAT WILL LEARN THAT WHEN IT SITS, IT GETS A TREAT, AND SOON IT'LL DO IT AUTOMATICALLY.

HOW TO TURN A NO INTO A YES

SOME ADULTS ARE NOT CRAZY ABOUT CATS - OR ANY PETS.

NO WAY.

HOWEVER, THERE ARE WAYS TO CHANGE A PARENT'S MIND.

1. BE REASONABLE. OFFER A WIDER VARIETY OF OPTIONS.

NO.

2. THINK OF THE REASONS WHY THE ANSWER IS NO, AND TRY TO WORK AROUND THEM.

IF SPACE IS A PROBLEM, THINK SMALL.

THE ANSWER'S STILL NO.

3. PROMISE YOUR PARENT YOU WILL LOOK AFTER YOUR PET.

HERE'S A SIGNED CONTRACT.

NO.

4. DO SOME CHORES TO EARN MONEY ...

... THEN OFFER TO HELP WITH THE COSTS OF YOUR PET.

NO!

5. AN EXTREMELY STUBBORN PARENT CALLS FOR MORE DRASTIC ACTION.

INTRODUCE A ROBOTIC PET TO YOUR PARENT.

DAD, THIS IS BUSTER.

SIT, BUSTER. NOW BEG!

TAKE YOUR PET FOR A WALK. DEMONSTRATE WHAT A RESPONSIBLE PET OWNER YOU WOULD BE.

WE'RE OFF TO THE PARK.

6. BUT IF IT DOESN'T WORK, DON'T DESPAIR. JUST WAIT A FEW WEEKS – THEN TRY AGAIN. PERSEVERANCE IS THE KEY.

PLAY WITH YOUR ROBOT PET AND MAKE SURE YOUR PARENT NOTICES HOW HAPPY IT MAKES YOU.

DAD, YOU REMEMBER BUSTER, DON'T YOU?

FETCH, BUSTER!

TOP TIPS FOR SPEECHMAKING

YOU'VE BEEN ASKED TO MAKE A SPEECH AT SCHOOL. DON'T BE SCARED OF SPEAKING IN PUBLIC – IT'S EASY IF YOU KNOW HOW.

TO MAKE THE BEST SPEECH YOU CAN, PLAN IN ADVANCE. ALLOW LOTS OF TIME TO PREPARE.

LEARN YOUR SPEECH BY HEART ...

... BECAUSE READING YOUR SPEECH FROM A PIECE OF PAPER WITHOUT LOOKING UP IS NOT AT ALL INTERESTING ...

... AND MAY CAUSE INJURY TO MEMBERS OF THE AUDIENCE.

AN INTERESTING SPEECHMAKER KEEPS HER COOL BY FOCUSING ON A FRIEND.

BUT DON'T STARE AT ONE PERSON FOR TOO LONG. EVERYONE IN THE AUDIENCE SHOULD FEEL INCLUDED.

HOW TO SURVIVE EMBARRASSMENT

AN EMBARRASSING MOMENT CAN HAPPEN WHEN YOU LEAST EXPECT IT, LIKE SHOWING UP TO A PARTY IN THE SAME DRESS AS A FRIEND.

THE TRICK IS HOW YOU GET OUT OF IT!
DON'T HIDE ...

... OR TRY TO COVER UP.

WHY NOT DO THIS INSTEAD?

HEY, I LIKE YOUR OUTFIT!

WHEN EMBARRASSMENT STRIKES, BE COOL, CALM, AND COLLECTED. HOLD YOUR HEAD UP HIGH AND SMILE!

HOW TO BE A MIND READER

TRY THIS TRICK WHEN YOU HAVE FREE TIME AT SCHOOL – IT COULD EVEN IMPRESS YOUR TEACHER!

WATCH ME READ MISS MOORE'S MIND.

GATHER EVERYONE AROUND YOU.

COME OVER HERE, EVERYONE.

IF THERE'S A HAT HANDY, GRAB IT. YOU'LL NEED IT IN A MINUTE.

IF NOT ... IT'S TIME TO IMPROVISE. YOU NEED SOMETHING THAT WILL HOLD SMALL PIECES OF PAPER.

ASK EVERYONE TO THINK OF A FAMOUS PERSON.

ASK EACH OF THEM TO TELL YOU THE NAME THEY'VE THOUGHT OF. WRITE EACH NAME DOWN ON A PIECE OF PAPER, FOLD IT TWICE, AND PUT IT IN THE HAT.

DON'T LET ANYONE SEE WHAT YOU'RE WRITING.

GET SOMEONE TO PICK A PIECE OF PAPER OUT OF THE HAT, BUT DON'T LET THEM OPEN IT.

NOW FOR A BIT OF ACTING ...

OOH, WHAT IS IT? IT'S COMING TO ME ...

HERE'S THE SECRET.

YOU WRITE THE SAME NAME DOWN ON EVERY PIECE OF PAPER!

WRITE DOWN OR TELL THEM THE NAME OF THE FAMOUS PERSON YOU THINK THEY PICKED — AND AMAZE THEM.

IS THIS THE NAME?

IT IS!

WARNING: ONLY TRY THIS ONCE — AND GET RID OF THE EVIDENCE FAST.

45

HOW TO SURVIVE A CRUSH

YOU'VE HAD A CRUSH ON A BOY FOR WEEKS AND WEEKS AND **WEEKS**, AND TODAY HE'S WALKING STRAIGHT TOWARD YOU. WHAT DO YOU DO?

1. KEEP CALM. REMEMBER, HE'S A PERSON, NOT A GOD.

2. IF HE ASKS YOU A QUESTION, TRY TO ANSWER IT ...

WHAT'S YOUR FAVORITE FOOD?

... SENSIBLY.

CHOC ... ER ... CHOC ... PIZZA.

CHOCOLATE PIZZA?

3. YOUR CRUSH WILL APPRECIATE YOU DOING **SOME** OF THE TALKING ...

... BUT NOT ALL OF IT.

4. DON'T STRETCH THE TRUTH TO APPEAR INTERESTING ...

TENNIS IS MY FAVORITE SPORT, TOO.

... BECAUSE YOU'LL PROBABLY GET FOUND OUT.

JUST BE YOURSELF.

5. EATING MESSY FOOD IN FRONT OF YOUR CRUSH CAN BE TRICKY, SO CHOOSE WISELY.

6. REMEMBER, IT'S GOOD TO GAZE INTO YOUR CRUSH'S EYES ...

... BUT WATCH WHERE YOU'RE GOING.

SEASIDE SURVIVAL

WANT TO BE A BEACH BEAUTY? HERE ARE
SEVEN IMPORTANT TIPS TO HELP YOU BECOME A SEASIDE SENSATION.

1. WHEN ON THE BEACH, LESS IS MORE – THE CASUAL LOOK IS DEFINITELY THE BEST.

2. CHOOSE A COMFORTABLE, WELL-FITTING BATHING SUIT. TOO TIGHT, AND YOU'LL SPEND YOUR TIME FIDGETING. TOO LOOSE, AND YOU MIGHT LOSE IT IF YOU ENCOUNTER ANY BIG WAVES.

3. WATCH OUT FOR WIND. BEACHES CAN BE GUSTY PLACES.

IT'S BEST TO TIE YOUR HAIR BACK, AND BE CAREFUL WHAT YOU WEAR.

HOW TO SOOTHE SUNBURN

IF YOUR SKIN IS SORE AND SUNBURNED, IT'S TIME TO CALL IN A RESCUE REMEDY.

HALF A CUP OF WARM WATER

HALF A CUP OF OATS

HONEY

PLAIN YOGURT

A MIXING BOWL

A TABLESPOON

LET THE OATS SOAK IN THE WATER FOR A FEW MINUTES.

THEN MIX IN TWO TABLESPOONS EACH OF HONEY AND YOGURT.

YOUR RESCUE REMEDY IS READY! JUST AVOID PUTTING IT NEAR YOUR EYES.

RELAX FOR 15 MINUTES, THEN RINSE IT OFF WITH WARM WATER.

RESULT!

DON'T FORGET THAT IT'S SAFEST NOT TO GET SUNBURNED IN THE FIRST PLACE. ALWAYS WEAR SUNSCREEN.

HOW TO PICK PERFECT SUNGLASSES

NO SUPERSTAR LEAVES THE HOUSE WITHOUT THE PERFECT PAIR OF SHADES. HERE'S HOW TO CHOOSE THE RIGHT ONES FOR YOUR FACE SHAPE.

FIRST, TAKE A GOOD LOOK AT YOUR FACE SHAPE IN THE MIRROR.

DRAW AROUND THE OUTLINE WITH LIPSTICK.

DON'T FORGET TO CLEAN IT OFF AFTERWARD.

PICK THE FACE SHAPE THAT MOST RESEMBLES YOURS TO FIND OUT WHAT SHAPE GLASSES WILL SUIT YOU.

ROUND: TRY BROAD FRAMES, AS WIDE AS YOUR FACE. SQUARE FRAMES LOOK GOOD, TOO.

HEART-SHAPED: DELICATE GLASSES OR FRAMELESS ONES WILL WORK.

SQUARE: TRY GENTLY CURVED SHAPES AND OVALS.

OVAL: YOU'RE LUCKY! EVERY SHAPE SHOULD WORK FOR YOU.

SURVIVING A
ZOMBIE ATTACK

IF ZOMBIES ATTACK, IT'S IMPORTANT TO ACT QUICKLY, BECAUSE JUST ONE BITE FROM A ZOMBIE COULD TURN YOU INTO ONE, TOO.

SPOTTING A ZOMBIE SHOULD BE PRETTY STAIGHTFORWARD.

A ROLLING HEAD

A CRAZY STARE

OUTSTRETCHED ARMS

A SLOW, STUMBLING WALK

IN THEORY, IT'S FAIRLY EASY TO KILL A ZOMBIE – BUT IN PRACTICE, AS ANY ZOMBIE FILM WILL DEMONSTRATE, IT'S NOT SO SIMPLE. READ ON TO DISCOVER HOW TO SURVIVE A ZOMBIE ATTACK.

DO NOT WASTE YOUR TIME WITH THE FOLLOWING:

SIT.

THEY CANNOT BE TRAINED ...

YOU WILL NOT BITE.

... OR HYPNOTIZED.

BUT DON'T DESPAIR. YOU HAVE ONE BIG ADVANTAGE OVER A ZOMBIE.

A BRAIN.

SO IF A ZOMBIE CORNERS YOU, OUTWIT IT. PRETEND TO BE A ZOMBIE, TOO. IF YOU CAN DROOL, EVEN BETTER.

HOW TO SPOT A FRENEMY

IT'S EASY TO RECOGNIZE YOUR TRUE FRIENDS. BUT FRENEMIES ARE OFTEN HARDER TO SPOT. HERE'S WHAT TO LOOK OUT FOR.

A FRENEMY MAKES YOU FEEL BAD MOST OF THE TIME.

SHE MIGHT MAKE JOKES AT YOUR EXPENSE ...

SHE'S SO SHORT, SHE'D FIT IN MY POCKET!

... OR NASTY COMMENTS.

WHAT ARE YOU WEARING?!

SHE MIGHT MAKE YOU FEEL STUPID.

YOU MUST BE THE CLUMSIEST GIRL IN SCHOOL.

BRILLIANT BOREDOM BUSTERS

ARE ALL YOUR FRIENDS BUSY? NOTHING TO DO?
DON'T DESPAIR, JUST READ ON ...

WHY NOT INCREASE YOUR BRAINPOWER? LEARN HOW TO SAY SOMETHING IN FIVE LANGUAGES.

MY BROTHER IS ANNOYING.

MON FRÈRE EST AGAÇANT.

OR LEARN SOMETHING BY HEART.

I WANDERED LONELY AS A CLOUD ...

THIS COULD BE THE DAY TO EARN EXTRA CASH ...

... OR TO LEARN A NEW SKILL.

WHY NOT TRY OUT A NEW HAIRSTYLE?

OR SORT OUT YOUR CLOTHES.

TOO SMALL.

TOO WORN.

TA DA!

AND IF YOU MANAGE TO FIND SOME FRIENDS, WHY NOT TRY MAKING YOUR OWN MUSIC VIDEO?

HOW TO SURVIVE TRUTH OR DARE

EVERYONE LOVES A GAME OF TRUTH OR DARE, BUT SOMETIMES IT'S TRICKY TO COME UP WITH GOOD IDEAS ON THE SPOT. HERE ARE SOME SUGGESTIONS FOR DEVILISH DARES TO GIVE YOUR FRIENDS.

1. PUT YOUR CLOTHES ON BACKWARD AND WEAR THEM TO SCHOOL.

2. TRICK YOUR TASTE BUDS WITH STRANGE FOOD. TRY CEREAL WITH ORANGE JUICE INSTEAD OF MILK.

3. RUN UP TO A BOY YOU DON'T KNOW AND TALK TO HIM.

4. SING YOUR FAVORITE SONG REALLY LOUDLY INSIDE A STORE.

5. TAKE YOUR PET PEBBLE FOR A WALK IN THE PARK.

COME ON, BOY.

1. WHAT'S THE BIGGEST LIE YOU'VE EVER TOLD?

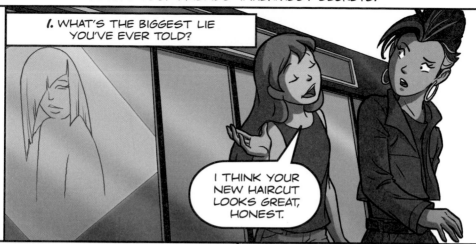

I THINK YOUR NEW HAIRCUT LOOKS GREAT, HONEST.

2. WHO IS YOUR SECRET CRUSH?

YOUR BROTHER!

3. WHAT'S THE MOST EMBARRASSING THING THAT HAS HAPPENED TO YOU?

4. WHAT WAS YOUR WEIRDEST DREAM ABOUT?

5. WHAT IS YOUR WORST HABIT?

SO GET READY TO GO HAVE FUN!

HOW TO BEAT BULLIES

BEING BULLIED? DON'T DESPAIR – BULLIES *CAN* BE BEATEN!

BULLIES ARE USUALLY COWARDS WHO PICK ON PEOPLE THEY THINK THEY CAN EASILY UPSET.

1. ALWAYS TELL SOMEONE – IT COULD BE YOUR MOM, A TEACHER, OR ANY ADULT YOU TRUST.

JUST SHARING THE PROBLEM MIGHT MAKE YOU FEEL BETTER ...

THANKS, MOM.

... AND IT'LL GIVE YOU TIPS FOR HOW TO DEAL WITH IT.

LET'S GO INTO SCHOOL AND TELL THEM WHAT'S BEEN HAPPENING.

2. KEEP A RECORD OF WHAT THE BULLY SAYS AND DOES AND WHEN THEY DO IT.

3. CYBERBULLYING CAN HAPPEN ONLINE, THROUGH E-MAILS AND INSTANT MESSAGES, OR ON SOCIAL NETWORKING SITES.

BUT IT'S STILL BULLYING, SO ALWAYS REPORT IT. NEVER RESPOND TO MESSAGES. BLOCK THE BULLY'S E-MAIL ADDRESS.

4. SURROUND YOURSELF WITH GOOD FRIENDS. GIRLS ON THEIR OWN ARE EASIER TARGETS. STOP BULLIES *BEFORE* THEY START.

5. IF A BULLY DOES PICK ON YOU, TRY TO LOOK AND SOUND CONFIDENT. YOU NEVER KNOW, IT MIGHT MAKE YOU *FEEL* CONFIDENT, TOO.

STAND UP TALL.

SPEAK SLOWLY.

HOLD YOUR HEAD UP HIGH WHEN YOU WALK AROUND.

USE A STRONG, CLEAR VOICE.

DON'T REACT OR SHOW THE BULLY THAT YOU'RE UPSET. SHE'LL JUST KEEP DOING IT IF SHE KNOWS IT GETS TO YOU.

NEVER FIGHT BACK. BE CALM AND REASONABLE. LOOK THE BULLY STRAIGHT IN THE EYE WHEN YOU TALK.

6. MOST IMPORTANT, NEVER *EVER* THINK BEING BULLIED IS YOUR FAULT. THE BULLY IS THE ONE WITH THE PROBLEM, NOT YOU.

HOW TO BE AN AMAZING BABYSITTER

BABYSITTING IS A FANTASTIC WAY TO EARN SOME EXTRA MONEY. HERE ARE SOME TIPS TO HELP YOU BECOME THE BEST BABYSITTER AROUND.

AN AMAZING BABYSITTER IS ALWAYS RIGHT ON TIME.

IT'S IMPORTANT TO ASK THE PARENTS SOME QUESTIONS BEFORE THEY GO OUT ...

CAN THEY HAVE SNACKS?

WHAT TIME DO THEY GO TO BED?

HOW CAN I CONTACT YOU?

... BECAUSE SMALL CHILDREN HAVE BEEN KNOWN TO EXAGGERATE.

MOM LETS US STAY UP UNTIL TEN.

SHE GIVES US CHOCOLATE IN BED ...

... EVERY SINGLE NIGHT.

IT'S A GOOD IDEA TO TIRE OUT THE KIDS BEFORE BEDTIME.

BUT REMEMBER TO CALM THINGS DOWN BEFORE BED OR THEY'LL NEVER GO TO SLEEP.

WHEN BEDTIME COMES, BE FIRM ...

... BUT KIND.

YES, YOU **DO** HAVE TO BRUSH YOUR TEETH.

I'LL LEAVE THE HALL LIGHT ON.

BABYSITTING CAN BE A GOOD TIME TO CATCH UP ON HOMEWORK.

BUT DON'T COUNT ON IT. SOMETIMES THINGS JUST DON'T WORK OUT.

NEVER IGNORE A PROBLEM. IT WON'T GO AWAY!

INSTEAD, TRY TO FIND A WAY TO SOLVE IT.

FLUFFY WANTS TO SLEEP NOW, JACK.

BECOME AN AMAZING BABYSITTER AND YOU'LL NEVER BE SHORT OF JOBS!

ALSO AVAILABLE ...

The Boys' Book: How to Be
the Best at Everything
978-0-545-01628-5

The Girls' Book: How to Be
the Best at Everything
978-0-545-01629-2